D1605585

how to survive today

*poems, prompts, and affirmations for those of us
still finding our way*

also by tonya ingram

Growl & Snare
Another Black Girl Miracle

poems, prompts,
& affirmations

for those
of us

still finding
our way

tonya ingram

First U.S. edition. Printed in the United States of America.

Wild Awake Publishing LLC
721 Depot Drive
Anchorage, Alaska 99501

ISBN: 978-1-7334637-6-8 (Paperback)
ISBN: 978-1-7334637-2-0 (Ebook)
1 2 3 4 5 6 7 8 9 19

wildawakepublishing.com

table of contents

dedication

this is for those of us who know the drum of mental health.
we also know the music of survival.
how to dance in the company of our thoughts.
how to be the most gorgeous story still being written.
how to survive today.

hello beautiful friend,

this book is a reminder of the goodness in being patient with yourself. the glory in being kind to your story. the magic in being ok with your process. my hope is that on the days you struggle to see yourself, this book will be the hug you need, the friend who listens, the reminder that you are not alone.

i love you, friend. i see you. i am proud of you.

thank you for showing up. thank you for staying.

p.s. - this is your book. write in it. tear pages out. do whatever feels right. i made this for you.

part 1: heartbreak

*there is space for your story, to sit by yourself
and be madly in love with the quiet.*

a note from tonya

at the end of 2017, i learned heartbreak.

this is the first photo i took when i left the relationship. or when
the relationship left me. the person who was once the center of
my world was no longer a resident of my heart. i had never felt
the power of being broken up with before. it turned my world, my
thoughts, my depression into disaster.

who was i without a lover?

who was i when i had to learn love for myself?

how to
deal with
heartbreak

know it is ok to miss someone who never deserved you. know it is ok to remember the good ol' days, the first kiss, the bar where you held each other, the memes you sent, the hours watching "Bob's Burgers." but it is also ok to block the number. to remember each time they unlearned your name on purpose. it is ok to give yourself a better joy, one where you come first. a joy where you do not have to carry a love that does not see you. a joy all too big for their small, small hate.

**for those
of us
who cry
ourselves
to sleep**

remember your magic. remember the thing most alive in you. remember the first time someone said "you're beautiful" and meant it. remember going to McDonald's and the ice cream machine actually working. remember when you didn't care what people thought of you. remember driving up the Pacific Coast Highway. remember tall grass and being held. remember it wasn't your fault. none of this wild river of sadness makes you any less deserving of a party in your honor. none of it minimizes your name or takes you away from yourself. and when you wake, remember the tears. what it is to bathe in a reminder that letting go is a healing you are ready to begin.

do not lose sleep on those who cannot love on your level. some people are afraid of heights.

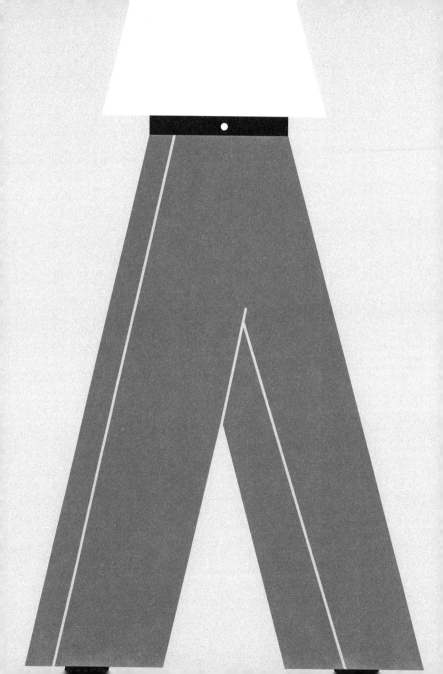

i want to be more than a good fuck. more than a body laid
out for the picking. for the feast. i want someone to take
me out of my clothes and my depression. i want to sleep
alongside them knowing i am not their morning shame.
not a woman who is usable but recyclable. good for now
but not good for the next day. i want more than what
you can put inside of me. for what can enter and leave so
quickly. so fast out the door, it calls me an Uber before i
put my shirt back on. i know the science of my heart. what
exhausts it. what good, good lovin' i can offer. i want more
than crying over another them. telling my friends the ex
ain't shit but still having to hold loneliness like a lover who
has yet to leave. i want more than the excuse of "it's me,
not you" when really it screams "i am selfish and cannot
admit it." i want to be a storm you dance in, not one you
watch from the inside of your room. comfortable and yet
still watered by my downpour. leave me to my peace, one
where you do not interrupt if you do not want to stay.

questions for my ex

after Mari Andrew

1. when did you know?
2. does it hurt when our song comes on?
3. where is the photo of me on the 4 train holding your favorite book? did you show them? did you delete it?
4. can they hold your breath in theirs and call that sacrifice?
5. what time was it when you stopped giving a fuck?
6. did it hurt when i loved you?
7. did it heal when i left you?
8. was it me?
9. can i let you go now?

they call me
difficult. i tell
them science
is difficult but
it still managed
to get a man on
the moon.

on the days you miss them, climb back into bed. order
your favorite takeout. turn on RuPaul's Drag Race. on the
days you miss your ex, avoid the photographs. avoid the
text messages. avoid the Facebook memories. remember
the first time you met. were you nervous? remember the
last time they said "i love you." did you trust it? remember
how they held your hand during chemotherapy, during
breakdowns, during times of unease. remember the gifts
you exchanged. the arguments that went on too long. the
resentment that made a home in miscommunication.
remember when they forgot your name, the way it needs
to be said. remember when they forgot the kind of person
you fight to be. it is ok to be the one who got away and
who wants to return. do not regret how big you love.
thunder does not lower its volume out of convenience.

do not guilt yourself for both hating and loving your ex. water can both freeze and pour. it does not lose its power in either.

on the days you feel lonely, what will you need?

fill in the circles with illustrations or words that represent those things.

to the ex: i led
you to the well,
and you did not
drink. i led myself
to the well, and i
have yet to thirst.

how to get over your ex

cry. cry. cry. cry. cry. cry. tears are like the rain, meant to release and cleanse. buy a coloring book. remind yourself of orange and violet and yellow and lime when everything feels gray. listen to anything by Adele. listen to "Bodak Yellow." in that order. volunteer at an animal shelter. hold a pet. know softness can be yours. cry. cry. cry. cry. cry. write the ex a letter. do not send it. write a letter to yourself. hide it. find it again when you need it most. plan a random adventure. buy the shoes or the extensions or the new video game. get lost in a bar or a library. Netflix will be the new bae. love accordingly. find time to scream, to be angry and present. keep the group chat close. it will be useful for the memes and the gossip and the "we are here for you." it is ok if you are still getting over it. it is ok to still cry. to work on believing in a love that is a radiance after the rain.

heartbreak is real but so are reruns of "The Office," naps
with your cat, and glasses of raspberry iced tea.
heartbreak is real but so is the thump of "what now?" in
your chest that is ready for a skyline beyond this coast. it is
the bed you no longer belong to. the Los Angeles you want
to sink your teeth into and figure it all out with. heartbreak
is real but so are the polaroids on the wall, the framed
moment you knew you could love outside of yourself. and
you did. you did. it will be ok. the view from the window
you look out of is but a film you have been led to direct.
you don't have to be perfect. you are not a tragedy
un-coached in the study of partnership. it didn't work out
and that is ok. there is space for your story, to sit by your-
self and be madly in love with the quiet.

write about where
your heart is.

_____

_____

_____

_____

_____

_____

_____

_____

_____

_____

_____

_____

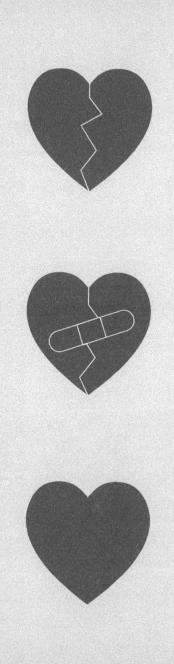

note to self:

do not exhaust your
heart on those who do not
want to invest in it.

**how to
be
single**

flirt with the sun. plan a vacation to
remind yourself of where you can go.
wear all of the booty shorts. learn how
to wink at the cutie from the beach,
from the bodega, from anywhere you be
stuntin'. download Tinder. delete Tinder.
download Tinder. delete Tinder. look in
the mirror and embrace your nude. buy
lingerie, not for the validation but for the
return of sexy like it never left. laugh at
your ex. laugh at hesitation. laugh at what
held you from yourself. let your lip gloss
be poppin'. let your earrings be glam.
respond to the "u up?" text if you want
to. send the "u up?" text if you want to.
be vocal about your glow up. put a spell
on your growth. tell it to stay, to be the
reminder of what you deserve. a love so
damn good it could only be something
you give yourself.

get you some friends who will tell you the ex, the date who
ghosted you, the person who cut you off in traffic ain't shit
and will take you out for frozen yogurt afterward. get you
some friends with loud mouths and louder hearts. get you
some friends who take photos of your good side. get you
some friends who keep it real. keep it sacred. get you some
friends who will protect your name in spaces that try to
destroy it. get you some friends with kindness in their DNA
and loyalty in their blood. get you some friends who will
let you know that shirt looks ridiculous with those shoes
and will honor your style regardless. get you some friends
who will visit you in the hospital. who stick around after
it is convenient. who will cheer you on after the curtains
close. the ones you can go days without speaking to and
pick up exactly where you left off. the kind of people who
help keep depression a quiet room. who sign the
declaration of your life that says you are the best fucking
thing to happen today.

I AM WORTHY OF LOVE

how to invite yourself to fall in love again

give your body a name it deserves. carve the dream into a tree, the dream you keep returning to. be the tune that reminds you of road trips and sand in between your toes. study your stretch marks. call each line a victory. a life you won. bathe in glitter and no fucks given. hit snooze on insecurity. tell anxiety it can't sit with us. devour what you crave and release expectation. buy the wig. buy the Taco Bell. buy the gift of being ok with the lonely. channel your inner Rihanna. stay hydrated. allow space for the weeping. allow yourself the hoe phase. allow acceptance to be its own parade. plant something. write a lullaby to the rain, to the sound of washing away. of letting go. call the homies and preach about the day you learned how to love yourself again.

for the next lover

there will be days i forget the
measurement of my worth. days i will
dive into the softest parts of myself. will
you know to hold my hand and play Janis
Joplin until weeping becomes the echo?
will you know Lunchables and hand-
holding make the heavy a noiseless song?
there will be days i string together
memories of the most ugly kind.
memories of ex-lovers with sharp
tongues. memories of those who touched
without consent. will you know to hold
me like the world is ending? like we met
under a meteorite with seconds to spare?
there will be days my body is not mine.
it will need repair. it will need chemo. it
will need rest. will you run your fingers
through my hair while it falls out? will you
trace my bad days and call it patience?
will you love me and love me and love me
better than the last mistake i made? i wait
for you. but until then i give myself this
magic, this love i call my own.

when you fall in love again

*inspired by
Nayyirah
Waheed*

when you fall in love again, let it be
messy. let it be lit. let it be life. let it be
the business. the sauce. the shit. on fleek.
on god. on everything. when you fall in
love again, let it cry your eyelashes off. let
it FaceTime you for hours. let it explain
to your best friends how cute this new
person is. let it give you wild thoughts and
a DJ Khaled key to life. when you fall in
love again, exclude the memories of your
ex. for each time you were gaslighted
because they could not love you out of
the dark. when you fall in love again, let
it harvest a kaleidoscope of butterflies. an
oil painting of the stomach drop you get
when they text you back. when you fall
in love again, let it be avocado toast and
farmer's market. the kind of bumbling
electricity that gets you out of the house.
out of a brawl with mental illness. when
you fall in love again, let it be passing
or forever. a coffee shop crush or a walk
down the aisle. water it. feed it. nourish
it. grow a love you can only give yourself,
one earthed in a reason to see you as
whole. as holy.

"after the breakup is the glow up."

- Mala Muñoz

after the breakup is the turn up, the bless up, the up and up. the ultralight beam. the choreography of "yass queen" taught to your body. after the breakup is the growth of your limbs, each part of you closer to the earth. the grand entrance. the main event. after the breakup is the shopping spree at Sephora, the dance classes no longer put off, the mansion of your heart finally able to open. after the breakup, shake it off. the sweat of your ex. the moments you were called crazy for daring to crawl outside of a love that was not a love. after the breakup is the marathon of whatever show gives you the drama you need. after the breakup is the birth of a you that was always present. always there. always marvelous in your waking and resting. a you that has learned a new language. a language that puts yourself first.

p.s. - if you can't love me at my 3PM glow,
you can't have me at my 3AM hoe.

hey friend, now it's your turn.

use the following pages to respond to the prompts
below or to write whatever is on your heart.
remember, this space is yours.

1. have you had someone walk out of your life?

2. who are you without that person?

3. who will you be when you learn love
for yourself?

put your
polaroid here.

part 2: self-love

you are your own affirmation,
a selfie for the gods.

a note from tonya

after heartbreak, i learned self-love is a process.

what did it mean to see myself as whole, especially after a loss? especially on the days i could barely get out of bed? i learned self-love is not neat. it is not linear. but it is mine. it is a selfie every day. it is an exploration. it is learning what beauty is for myself and learning to find my worth outside of someone else.

it is labor to say you are worthy of a love so grand it gives life to all of the dead things that made a home in your heart. it is labor to say "i am beautiful" and mean it. to look into the reflection and call the person looking back at you a miracle. a story unfinished and glorified. a canvas with a thousand stars. a lullaby made for the gods. it is labor to not scrub the black off your skin because of what you were told it makes of you. to be in the body you call home when it feels like the wrong address. to love when you do not understand it. it is labor to feel sexy without apologizing for it. to get the degree. to leave your legs unshaved. to quit the job. to give it all you are made of. did the forecast not give a kiss to the start of your day? did the dirt not ask for a dance when it met you? you are so perfect. so fragile. so kicking and screaming. this is your labor. this is your birth. everything in the world holds its arms out for you.

note to self:

this is the year people will walk out of your life. don't worry. they are moving out so it will be easier for you to clean the house, remove the clutter, and say "this is mine. you are no longer welcome here."

today i declare independence from insecurity and biting my nails and giving a shit about their opinion. today i declare independence from my mistakes. the ones dressed in a regret. today i declare independence from comparison and overpriced apples and sparkling water. today i declare independence from the ex and the remarkable moment of finding love and losing it. i declare independence from the "u up" texts, from fear and its big mouth, from stank breath and movies where i can predict the ending. today i declare my joy. a chicken-with-rice-and-beans joy. a laughing-so-hard-i-cry joy. a patient-with-myself joy. a joy that is a standing ovation i finally accept.

i will no longer beg for anyone to love me. a tree does not beg and still offers the sweetest fruit to those willing to reach for it.

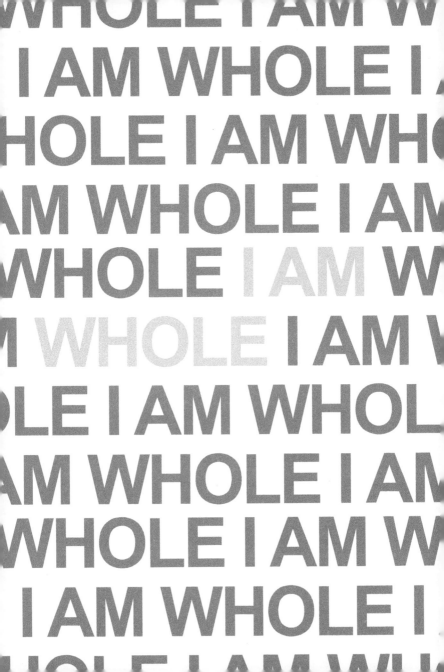

how to
be alone

find a book. a story made of escape. a story to widen the smile. leave the
headphones behind and wander. wander into the thrift shop. the flower shop.
your heart shop. spend too many hours in Target. price your favorite lamp
and come back to it. let it be a reminder that you are worthy of light. learn
the meaning of your name, the one you want to be called. find a forest and
a moment to give thanks. daydream without restriction. fart. sing your favor-
ite Broadway musical off-key. buy a balloon and write about a romance that
left you breathless, then let it go. make room for a new memory. for a peace
undeniably yours. build a fort. welcome your insecurities. tell them to rest. to
take a break. pray for a loneliness that does not hurt. pray for a loneliness like a
stream. like a cuddle. like the last time someone broke your heart but not your
story. alone is not a chorus. alone is an encore we give ourselves to keep from
fading.

be patient with
the blooming of
your heart.

shoutout to those of us who get it wrong way more than
we get it right. shoutout to the dropout and the laid
off. the constant wedgie-haver and the forever-stressed
entertainer. shoutout to the not today-ers and the alarm
clock-snoozers. shoutout to the train/bus-missers and the
coffee-spillers. to those who did not shower today. shoutout
to the face-in-pillow godsends, the cry-over-anything
champions. to those constantly stuck in traffic. to the FML
mascots and the bad date reminders. to the eye-rollers and
teeth-suckers. shoutout to the embarrass-yourself-in-front-
of-your-crush-and-accidentally-butt-dial-your-ex winners.
to the ran-out-of-toilet-paper and the over-30-unread-
messages captains. perfection is overrated. it is not your
job to be cruel to the process. it is your job to be patient
with it.

for so many
of us, being able
to show up today is
the best we can do.
do not call it
drowning. we are
simply learning how
to walk on water.

honor your imperfections. honor the birthmark on the side
of your face. the inability to tell your left from your right.
how horrible you are at giving directions. honor the short-
comings. the reasons for failing the test. honor the defeat.
the game-winning shot you missed. the ex you keep going
back to. the moment you told yourself no more and res-
urrected a lie. honor the drools, the wedgies, the constant
tripping over your feet. honor the weeping. the unknown
name of your father. the doctor's note. the journey that
may not be perfect but is yours. thank goodness for how
sensitive you are. how you shine. thank goodness for each
flaw. for each thing trying to work against you not knowing
it is working for you.

a reminder to those of us who feel insignificant

you are made of stardust. you are a galaxy reborn. take sight. look up. the love thumpin' in your heart's radio is infinite. you, small radiant planet. you, bursting, full moon. you are an earth poem, an unending story of *how did you get here* and *who was your first love* and *what scares you most*. take sight. look up. it is ok to abandon the day and be as still as the North Star or as big as Jupiter. you are wondrous and something to be marveled at. you are a sight to see.

even on the days
i am the most
terrified, i will know
my name to be the
loudest truth in
the sky.

stop apologizing for the space you take up. the sun is not sorry for its rise.

because i love myself,
i will not accept:

i will not accept _____

i will not accept _____

i will not accept _____

i will not accept _____

i will not accept _____

i will not accept _____

i will not accept _____

i will not accept _____

i will not accept _____

i will not accept _____

i will not accept _____

i will not accept _____

note to self:

you are worth someone's time,
including your own. it is ok to cancel
plans. do not feel guilty for taking
care of yourself.

take yourself out on a date. reserve a table for one. say yes
to retail therapy. go to the movies alone. become lost in a
story that is not your own but is yours for the departure.
sign up for the boxing class, the salsa class, the swimming
class, the i-am-falling-in-love-with-myself-every-damn-
day-class. write it down. your goals. the guide on how to
claw your way out of stress, out of the heavy that keeps
you hurting. keep the playlist on repeat, the one to cradle
a long day. the one to soothe the ache in your bones. to
remind you of your growing heart. learn your birth chart.
sit in a park with your favorite book. bring grapes. leave
your phone. be in your body. hold each word like a sacred
spell. solitude can be a friend. can be the sweetest hum
when everything is rattle and wreck.

how to be sexy

serve face to doubt. apply winged eyeliner
for every day you choose to stay. really
believe that it is ok if the jeans don't fit.
know that there is no shame in growth.
wear the crop top. the pasties. the bikini.
let your stomach be the glory. let your
savage be Fenty. embrace the
constellation of freckles. be naked. be
unapologetically naked. flirt with your
insecurities. the bitten nails. the gap
tooth. the mole. eat whatever the hell you
want. record your reason to keep going.
follow the instructions of your fierce.
compliment your damn self. fuck
competition. sexy is inclusion. it is the
reflection you return to. the slay
unbothered.

note to self:

have a crush on your
own damn self.

now sing a love song to yourself

praise your feelings. the overexcitement when the food
finally arrives. when the parking ticket is forgiven. when
the rice is cooked properly. decorate the inside of your
giggle. the complexity of your sadness. celebrate the
advice you give but cannot take. the number you have yet
to delete. the phone you just dropped. the anger at the
wifi not working. the confusion of being ghosted. take it
in. the dance of emotion. the gala of feels. acknowledge
that failure is not a production but a process. none of it
requires the dulling of your power. none of it makes you
less of a monument. your signature is on the sunrise of
today. celebrate.

a love lost is not always a love returned, but a love you give yourself will always be a love worth keeping.

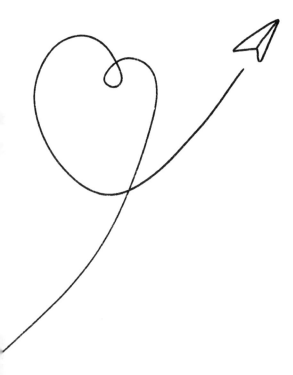

p.s. - send an invitation to your heart.
ask it to come home.

hey friend, now it's your turn.

use the following pages to respond to the prompts
below or to write whatever is on your heart.
remember, this space is yours.

1. how do you define beauty?

2. how do you define your worth?

3. what does your process of self-love look like?

put your
polaroid here.

part 3: healing, then joy

it's the small things.
a construction of hope. a house of abundance.
everything good greeting you at the door
and welcoming you home.

a note from tonya

through self-love, i learned how to be kind to myself.

how to look at my reflection and be ok with each flaw,
each failure. this is what healing looks like. it is not a race
to the finish. it is not convincing myself i am better when
i know better is a navigation, not a destination. healing is
the story i am writing. it is the joy i am growing into.

how to
be strong

don't. be a hot mess. an ugly cry in the emergency room. the third rejection letter this week. ruin your makeup while weeping over the unpaid parking ticket. the overdue phone bill. download OkCupid immediately after the ex you met on OkCupid leaves you. borrow a shoulder to lean on and a Spotify playlist to lose your voice to. find a bubble bath after dialysis. find a cute dog after an anxiety attack. find your name after you were called out of it. write a love poem to the day you could not get out of bed. laugh at the negative balance in your bank account. be bold about your fears. about the diagnosis. about the day you thought you would not make it. strength is an occupation. a marigold in dust. a thing we cannot see when the world is ending but a reminder we keep when we survive long enough to see that it has not.

it is ok to be the draft. the unfinished. the still-working-on-it. the not yet. to hang up on the bill collector. to sweat in places that you "shouldn't" sweat. to ask someone to prom and get rejected. it is ok to pile your uncertainties. to run into a glass door. to define alone as a song you wrote for yourself. it is ok to not have the words. to shut the blinds and collect the sadness. to hydrate, deactivate, and meditate, in that order. to be afraid of how the next one will handle your heart. it is ok to give side-eye and deep breath because there was once a day like the one you are having and you made it out of that one. remember that. it is ok to be constantly in the making.

sometimes you have to remind yourself that you are doing enough. sometimes you have to rest. sometimes you have to quit with the comparisons. sometimes you have to log off. sometimes you have to run away. to a friend's couch. to the ears of someone who will listen. sometimes you have to get lost to know where you are going. sometimes you have to isolate. take a break. find the silence. sometimes you are best developed when you are most unsure. everything in the wind whistles "you are needed" despite the crash of your heart and the bend of your hope. know that you are exactly where you need to be, under the clouds and in love with yourself.

how to deal with anxiety

greet the morning. there is a dawn with your name on it. seek the ocean and a bowl of strawberries. paint your face in opulence and unbothered swag. ask someone for the Netflix, Hulu, HBO passwords. find those who will hold your heart and not rattle it. be ok with being rattled. let the breeze bring you home. bring you every good thing you have to say about yourself. quiet the voice that tells you otherwise. people-watch. read anything but the news. examine the dance in those who call today a miracle. today is beautiful even in its bullshit. bless the breath that keeps you. bless the shot of whiskey and the club you find yourself lost in. lay down and look up. cry. curse. whisper "this too shall pass" even if you don't believe it yet. the universe will hear you. will lend its planets in celebration of you. will tell the stars your story. how you got here. how you survive.

find fewer ceilings and more sky. there is so much beyond right now.

today is one of those days. one of those leave-me-
alone-as-i-eat-an-entire-pizza days. one of those
if-another-person-on-Bumble-asks-where-i-live-before-
they-ask-how-i-am-i-am-going-to-lose-it days. one of
those five-loads-of-laundry-waiting-to-be-done days.
one of those electric-bouts-of-lonely days. one of those
fierce-waves-of-sadness days. one of those dammit-
i-am-a-catch-and-still-single days. one of those mis-
matched-socks-and-hole-in-t-shirt days. one of those
phone-battery-constantly-on-5% days. one of those i-have-
not-talked-to-my-mom-in-days days. one of those i-need-
to-forget-my-ex's-number days. one of those Beyon-
cé's-"Lemonade"-on-repeat days. not the whole album,
just the angry shit. today is one of those days. but today is
also the day i make it. and today i make time for me.

none of this is against you. the groceries you dropped
while trying to get your keys. the traffic you are stuck in.
the person who won't text you back. the mosquito bite on
your left elbow. the rain you did not bring an umbrella for.
no, you are not busy chaos or open flaw. the extraordinary
happens when we stop looking for it. the train you just
missed. the diagnosis. the love you lost. it got you here.
with a lot learned and a damn good story. sometimes that
is all we can ask for. sometimes that is enough.

how to start to believe you are enough

sing your favorite song. loudly, softly, like it is gospel. whisper into the resting of your palms. say "magic" and the thought of your ex will disappear. drink water. plenty. enough to make an ocean of your brilliance. enough to fill the room in which joy forgot it was alive in you. dance. in a T-rex costume. in the middle of a flash flood without shoes but with an enormous amount of heart. say "fuck you" to the running of anxiety. say "yes" to the inhale of self-forgiveness. it is medicine. it is comfort unlike the kind you received from a selfish love. write a poem. not for the audience but for the construction of your breath. a to-do list for those of us who forget our worth. call up the homie. tell them it is a reunion. tell them today is shit but you are a head nod to the sky. a force unshakeable. write a note to worry. tell it staying is not an option. take in anything with comedy spilling from its story. be ok. be ok with not being ok. go to the mirror. close your eyes. say your name, softly. say it again. like Missy Elliot is featured on the track. like trauma is in the backseat today. open your eyes. repeat.

i want to make mistakes. bold, unruly mistakes. i want to scrape my knee while learning how to skateboard. i want to make out on the dance floor. give me face-in-palm truth. give me stunning fault. i want to stay out too late. i want to fail the exam. come on, luxurious error. i want to move to the wrong city. i want to bite my nails and burp at the dinner table. there is nothing honest about perfection. there is no growth in comfort. hold me, misguided heart. bring me home, righteous wrong. i want to learn the dance of thriving. how to fall on my face and be in love with every scar.

note to self:

stay with me.
i'm working on it.

how to heal

think of the heartbreak. the doctor's visit. the day you wished was over. remember how small the world felt. how easy it was to not return to yourself. marvel at your hands for everything they open. light a candle. recite Michelle Obama. make a smoothie. fill it with the fruits of your ancestors. with a sweetness worth keeping. block the account. do not look at the photo of your ex and their new love at the beach. on the grass. in where you failed. instead tell yourself you belong here. to the church of Lizzo and better days. open the windows and put away the laundry. there is a buffet of possibilities with your name on it. a bed of pillows waiting for your arrival. healing is not linear. not a competition. it is all we hold sacred. how we call on tomorrow while leaning on today.

today is a new day. today is the morning after the empty. the eggs scrambled perfectly. the car not breaking down. today is the do-over. the second chance. the grace in fucking up and then getting it right. today you are not the stuck, not the unpretty. today you are a Kendrick Lamar lyric, a Nina Simone howl. you are your own affirmation, a selfie for the gods. today is not the alarm and its many snoozes. not the parked car you walked into. not the ex and the fragile memories. today you are daffodil and honey. the turn-up and the grateful. today is a supernova. a holy grail. a beauty mark. it is new. meaning it is yours. despite the dirt you crawled through to get here. how much of it covers you. all of it a reason to grow. to blossom. to say "watch me push through."

what do you need to give yourself permission for?

dear _____ ,

today i give you permission to:

_____

_____

_____

_____

love,

_____

how to survive today

it's the small things. the extra fries at the bottom of the bag. the 50% off sale with no exclusions. the nail not chipping. each time you drop your phone and there is no crack. the bass of your grandmother's laughter. Cardi B getting her entire life. going through checkout and your card not being declined. a hot shower. someone to text. stretching your back. making no time for the bullshit. the brows no longer sisters but twins. the dinner you don't have to pay for. the dj playing the one song you've been singing all day. making it home safely. the symptoms finally quiet. the doctor with good news. the house to yourself. it's the small things. a construction of hope. a house of abundance. everything good greeting you at the door and welcoming you home.

i will survive for:

_____   _____

_____   _____

_____   _____

_____   _____

_____   _____

_____   _____

_____   _____

_____   _____

_____   _____

_____   _____

_____   _____

_____   _____

_____   _____

i will be so damn
alive that it scares
the doubt in me.

I WILL
THRIVE

**how to
make
room
for joy**

book a flight. select the window seat.
remind yourself that you belong to the
sky and everything beneath it. grab the
basketball and practice your jump shot.
remember that we learn best from the
shots we miss. drink ginger tea. drink a
shot of tequila. eat all of the sourdough
bread. grab the quilt and let it hug your
body. let it give you a warmth on the
days the chill feels impossible to shake.
give yourself light instead. sit in a gar-
den with nothing but your exhale and
a breeze, a brush from the wind. listen
to Jacob Banks. let the music bring you
home. clip your toenails. spell freedom
with your favorite memory and not an
ode to guilt. put shame on silent. shower
in cocoa butter bubble bath soap and
patience for yourself. dance. two-step.
pop your back. sweat the insecurity out.
polish your nails in the brightest tri-
umph. remember your body. remember
hydration is not just about the water we
drink but the water we return to. find
what calls you. give it your name. whis-
per to the earth a secret. make space for
tears. for failure. for confusion. because
after the flood comes the knowing. a
validation that was always yours.

let nothing

i fled the
sadness and
made a home in
my rebuilding.
made a joy
out of chaos.
made a name
worth keeping.

p.s. - do not apologize for how long it took for you
to heal. a bird is not sorry for being born with the
inability to take flight. it requires practice to soar.

this is what joy looks like.

after the storm comes the calm. after healing comes the joy.
i found my laughter again. i learned my name. i ate until i
was full. i forgave myself again and again. i held myself.
i guess that is joy. everything i was no longer apologetic for
but everything my heart was ready to receive.

hey friend, now it's your turn:

use the following pages to respond to the prompts
below or to write whatever is on your heart.
remember, this space is yours.

1. what does healing look like to you?

2. what does joy look like to you?

3. what does your story look like now?

put your
polaroid here.

resources

i know you may be struggling right now. that's ok. there's no shame in asking for help, which is why t compiled this list of resources for you. it isn't comprehensive, but it does contain information about a few organizations i support that you might find helpful.

please get the help you need. i believe in you, friend.

American Foundation for Suicide Prevention

Established in 1987, the American Foundation for Suicide Prevention is a voluntary health organization that gives those affected by suicide a nationwide community empowered by research, education, and advocacy to take action against this leading cause of death.

www.afsp.org

Crisis Text Line

Crisis Text Line is free, 24/7 support for those in crisis. Text HOME to 741741 from anywhere in the US to text with a trained Crisis Counselor.

www.crisistextline.org

National Alliance on Mental Illness

The National Alliance on Mental Illness is the nation's largest grassroots mental health organization dedicated to building better lives for the millions of Americans affected by mental illness.

www.nami.org

Project LETS

Project LETS builds peer-led communities of support, education, and advocacy for folks with lived experience of mental illness, trauma, Disability, and/or neurodivergence. They believe that principles of Disability Justice are key components to supporting collective healing and our human rights.

www.letserasethestigma.com

Project UROK

An initiative of the Child Mind Institute, Project UROK is an inclusive community with expert mental health resources for teens and young adults who are committed to ending the stigma and isolation of struggling with mental illness.

www.projecturok.org

Therapy for Black Girls

Therapy for Black Girls is an online space dedicated to encouraging the mental wellness of Black women and girls. So often the stigma surrounding mental health issues and therapy prevent Black women from taking the step of seeing a therapist. Dr. Joy Harden Bradford developed the space to present mental health topics in a way that feels more accessible and relevant.

www.therapyforblackgirls.com

The Trevor Project

Founded in 1998 by the creators of the Academy Award®-winning short film TREVOR, The Trevor Project is the leading national organization providing crisis intervention and suicide prevention services to lesbian, gay, bisexual, transgender, queer, and questioning (LGBTQ) young people under 25.

www.thetrevorproject.org

To Write Love on Her Arms

TWLOHA is a nonprofit movement dedicated to presenting hope and finding help for people struggling with depression, addiction, self-injury, and suicide.

www.twloha.com
www.twloha.com/find-help

acknowledgments

thank you, God.

to the family i was given: my mother, my sister vanessa, my brothers charles and tony, my grandparents, and my uncle. thank you for being the reason i know joy. thank you for being my first examples of love.

to the family I choose: Alyesha Wise-Hernandez and Matthew "Cuban" Hernandez. thank you for being my home, my favorite inside jokes, my Marvel fanatics, my "The Price is Right" team, and my fam always.

to the Barnes family: thank you for everything.

to my cheetah sisters, my coven, my best friends: Dr. Laryssa Green, Janelle Renee Pearson, and Olivia J. Holloway. you have taught me how to be kind to myself, how to trust my heart, how to be present even when it's difficult. thank you for your magic. thank you for your sisterhood. thank you for our Korean bbq dates.

to my mentor: Shihan Van Clief. thank you for checking on me when i didn't check on myself. thank you for believing in me when i don't believe in myself.

to Suzanne Lacy: i know resilience because of you. how to name my brilliance and swim in it.

to my publisher, Jennie Armstrong, and my editor, Claire M. Biggs: We did it, y'all. thank you for seeing something in me, my words, and my story. thank you for your beautiful patience, your wild ideas, and your inspiring optimism. i dream a little bigger because of you.

a special shoutout to To Write Love on Her Arms for how much you have invested in me, for how much you have helped me on days i barely knew how to help myself.

to every light who donated, paid a hospital visit, sent a message, shared a poem, or told me their story: i write for you. you have taught me how to show up and how to keep showing up. thank you to the moon and beyond.

lastly, to every beautiful person who found a home in my words, who has extended their friendship, who i call friend: i love you.

wild awake publishing

books you can ~~lose~~ find yourself in.

www.wildawakepublishing.com

instagram: @readwildawake

about the author

Tonya Ingram is a poet, Cincinnati native, Bronx-bred introvert, mental health advocate, kidney transplant hopeful, Lupus legend, cat auntie, and lover of Tom Hardy and "The Office."

Tonya has graced the stages of The Getty Museum, Madison Square Garden, San Francisco Opera House, Nuyorican Poets Café, The John F. Kennedy Center for the Performing Arts, Lexus Verses and Flow's variety show, and "The Price is Right*," the online and physical pages of The New York Times, Vice i-D, Bustle, and Marie Claire, and the classrooms of schools in the United States and Ghana, just to name a few. Her viral collaboration with BuzzFeed, "An Open Letter to My Depression," has reached over 4 million views and counting.

A friend, creative, daydreamer, and Virgo, Tonya's writing explores the necessity in taking care of ourselves, especially on the days we feel unworthy. She is a graduate of New York University and Otis College of Art and Design. Tonya currently resides in Los Angeles, CA.

How To Survive Today is her third book of poetry.

You can find her on Instagram (@tonyainstagram), Twitter (@TonyaSIngram), and on her website (www.tonyaingram.com).

She won.

CPSIA information can be obtained
at www.ICGtesting.com
Printed in the USA
LVHW071555140820
662262LV00004BA/16

9 781733 463768